THE LITTLE
CITRUS
COOKBOOK

CATHERINE PHIPPS

Photography by Mowie Kay

Hardie Grant

QUADRILLE

Managing Director: Sarah Lavelle
Assistant Editor: Sofie Shearman
Designer: Emily Lapworth
Photographer: Mowie Kay
Food stylist: Marina Filippelli
Prop Stylist: Iris Bromet
Copy Editor: Sally Somers
Head of Production: Stephen Lang
Senior Production Controller: Sabeena Atchia

First published in 2023 by Quadrille,
an imprint of Hardie Grant Publishing

Quadrille
52–54 Southwark Street
London SE1 1UN
quadrille.com

Text © Catherine Phipps 2023
Photography © Mowie Kay 2017
Design and layout © Quadrille 2023

Text is extracted and updated from *Citrus*
by Catherine Phipps.

Cataloguing in Publication Data: a
catalogue record for this book
is available from the British Library.

ISBN: 978 1 83783 025 1

Printed in China

CONTENTS

SOUPS, SALADS AND SMALL PLATES 4

MAIN COURSES 30

SIDE DISHES 58

SOMETHING SWEET 70

PRESERVES AND DRINKS 98

INDEX 110

SOUPS, SALADS AND SMALL PLATES

LIME AND CHICKEN
TORTILLA SOUP

Serves 4

**For the chicken and
  marinade**

2 boneless, skinless
chicken breasts,
butterflied

Finely grated zest and juice
of 1 lime

1 tsp each of chipotle chilli
powder, garlic powder
and dried oregano

½ tsp smoked salt

1 tbsp olive oil

For the soup

2 tbsp olive oil

1 red onion, finely diced

2 red (bell) peppers, finely
diced

2 celery sticks, finely diced

500g/1lb 2oz very ripe
tomatoes

1 head of garlic, broken
into cloves

1 chipotle chilli, whole but
deseeded

continued...

**This has quite a lot of elements to it and ends up being
a bit of an assembly job towards the end. It's not a true
tortilla soup (I don't like soggy tortillas, much better to
have them as a crisp garnish), more of a cross between
that and *sopa de lima*. You can play around with the
garnishes as much as you want. Crumbled feta – which
is really a salty version of the Latin American *queso
fresco* – would work instead of a hard cheese, as would a
traditional guacamole in place of the avocado.**

Put the chicken breasts in a bowl. Mix together the
marinade ingredients and pour this over the chicken. Leave
to marinate for 1 hour. Heat a griddle pan until it is too hot
to hold your hand over. Griddle the chicken for 3–4 minutes
on each side until just cooked through. Set aside.

Heat the oil for the soup in a large flameproof casserole or
saucepan. Add the onion, red (bell) peppers and celery. Sauté
on a low heat until translucent and starting to caramelize
lightly. This will take at least 10–15 minutes. Meanwhile,
put the tomatoes, unpeeled garlic cloves and chilli in a
heavy-based frying pan and dry roast for a similar amount
of time until the tomatoes are blackening. If the chilli and
garlic look done before the tomatoes, fish them out and put
to one side. Peel the garlic cloves and put in a food processor
with the unpeeled tomatoes and chilli. Blitz until smooth.

continued...

3 tbsp finely chopped coriander (cilantro) stems (save leaves for garnish)

A large sprig of thyme

1 litre/generous 4 cups chicken stock

200g/generous 1 cup cooked black beans (optional)

For the garnishes

1 avocado

Juice of 1 lime

2–3 tbsp olive oil

2–3 corn tortillas, cut into triangles

100ml/7 tbsp soured cream

A few coriander (cilantro) leaves

Grated hard cheese, such as Manchego, Gruyère or Cheddar (or see intro on page 6)

Add the coriander (cilantro) stems and thyme sprig to the onion pan and cook for a couple of minutes. Pour in the tomato mixture and simmer for 5 minutes until starting to reduce. Add the chicken stock and continue to simmer for around 15–20 minutes.

For the garnishes, dice the avocado and toss in the lime juice. Heat the oil in a large frying pan and fry the tortilla triangles until crisp and golden brown. Shred the chicken and add it to the soup along with the black beans, if using. Remove the thyme sprig and serve the soup garnished with the tortillas, avocado, soured cream, coriander (cilantro) leaves and cheese.

CHICKEN, CHARD AND GIANT COUSCOUS SOUP

Serves 4

1 tbsp olive oil

1 tbsp butter

2 leeks, cut into thin rounds

2 garlic cloves, finely chopped

Finely grated zest of 1 lemon or lime

A bunch of chard, leaves only, shredded

50g/1¾oz yellow beans, halved

50g/1¾oz runner beans, halved

1 litre/generous 4 cups well-flavoured chicken stock

200g/7oz cooked giant couscous (about 60g/2oz uncooked weight)

200g/7oz cooked chicken, torn into chunks

Sea salt and freshly ground black pepper

A few shavings of Parmesan, to serve (optional)

continued...

This soup started out as a collection of leftovers in my refrigerator – the first time I made it, the cooked chicken had a subtle aroma of bergamot. Citrus delicately pervades the soup, but the harissa-style dressing really adds another dimension to the flavour. It's a bit like adding pistou to minestrone.

Heat the olive oil and butter in a large saucepan or flameproof casserole. When the butter has melted, add the leeks with a splash of water and season with salt and pepper. Cover and cook very gently for 10 minutes, checking every so often, until tender and buttery. Add the garlic and cook for a further couple of minutes, trying not to stir too much.

Add the zest, chard leaves and beans, then pour over the stock. Bring to the boil then reduce the heat and simmer for a few minutes until the beans are tender, then add the couscous and chicken. Continue to simmer just to warm through.

continued...

For the harissa dressing

25g/1½ cups fresh parsley
  leaves

10g/¾ cup fresh mint
  leaves

10g/¾ cup fresh coriander
  (cilantro) leaves

½ tsp ground cardamom

½ tsp ground fennel seed

½ tsp ground coriander

1 garlic clove, crushed

1 green chilli (optional)

1 tbsp preserved lemon
  or lime (see page 100
  for homemade)

50ml/3½ tbsp olive oil

Juice of ½ lemon or 1 lime

A few fresh lemon verbena
  leaves (optional)

While the soup is simmering, make the harissa dressing. Simply put everything in a food processor and blitz until you have a fresh-looking green paste – you may have to thin with a little water if you are finding it recalcitrant. Taste for seasoning and add salt if necessary.

Serve the soup with spoonfuls of the dressing stirred in at the last minute, with a few shavings of Parmesan, if you like.

DEEP-FRIED
CITRUS SLICES

Serves 4

2–3 citrus fruits (a variety is good)

100ml/7 tbsp buttermilk

75g/generous ½ cup plain (all-purpose) flour

25g/1 tbsp semolina or fine cornmeal

A neutral-tasting oil, such as groundnut or sunflower, for deep-frying

To serve

Pinches of:

Smoked chilli (chipotle) or hot smoked paprika (for lime slices)

Herbes de Provence or za'atar (for orange slices)

Fennel pollen or sumac (for lemon slices)

continued...

The idea for these comes from one of my favourite cookbooks, *The Zuni Café Cookbook* by the late Judy Rodgers. They are so unexpectedly moreish that there is a fine argument for eating them on their own, with just a sprinkle of salt – do try them that way at least once. But there are other things that do enhance the flavour. Lemon is good with a fine sprinkling of sumac or fennel pollen, lime loves a dash of smoked chilli or cayenne, whilst orange I like with herbes de Provence or za'atar.

I don't always bother with an accompaniment for these, but when I do, I make this yogurt dip. You can replace the fennel with any of the flavour suggestions mentioned above, or indeed anything else you fancy.

If serving with the dip (overleaf), make this first – simply mix everything together and season with salt and pepper.

Top and tail the citrus fruit to the point where you get a good showing of flesh as opposed to pith and skin. Slice the fruit as finely as possible while keeping each slice intact, removing any pips.

Put the buttermilk in a bowl. Put the flour and semolina onto a plate and season with salt and pepper, then whisk briefly to combine and get rid of any lumps.

Dip the citrus slices in the buttermilk and shake or lightly scrape them to get rid of any excess. Drop the slices onto the flour mixture and give the plate a little shake. Flip over and repeat. Dust off any excess – you don't want a thick coating as you want to see the detail from the citrus through the batter.

continued...

**For the yogurt dip
(optional)**

250ml/generous 1 cup
Greek yogurt

1 tsp fennel seeds, crushed

A pinch of sugar

A squeeze of lemon juice

Sea salt and freshly ground
black pepper

Heat enough oil for deep-frying in a heavy-based saucepan
or fryer to about 180°C/350°F. Fry the slices a few at a time
– when they start to go golden brown remove with a slotted
spoon to a plate lined with kitchen paper. The slices will
continue to brown once they are removed and will be nicely
caramelized in patches.

Sprinkle with salt, then the corresponding spices and/or
herbs for each fruit and serve with yogurt dip, if you like.

SEA BASS CEVICHE

Serves 4

2 small, sweet oranges

1 small red onion, thinly sliced

600g/1lb 5oz extremely fresh sea bass, placed in the freezer for 30 minutes

100g/3½oz small tomatoes, preferably yellow/orange, cut into quarters

A few small coriander (cilantro) leaves

A few small basil leaves

For the tiger's milk

2.5cm/1-in piece of fresh root ginger, sliced

1 fat garlic clove, squashed

A few coriander (cilantro) stems, bruised

100ml/7 tbsp lime juice (or sour orange juice)

½ Scotch bonnet chilli, finely chopped, plus extra to serve

A few thyme sprigs, bruised

Sea salt

One period of my working life was spent researching Peruvian food, and out of this came a mild obsession with what is known as "*leche de tigre*", or tiger's milk. This is a purée of citrus and chilli that is used to "cook" the fish to its ceviched state – the remains are often drunk in shot glasses or used in cocktails. Lime is the usual citrus in ceviche, but you can also use sour orange juice.

This recipe has a Caribbean flavour, as I love the taste and aroma of Scotch bonnet chillies.

Segment the oranges: top and tail the citrus and sit it firmly on your chopping board. Then cut from top to bottom, following the contour of the fruit, making sure you are cutting away the pith and outer membrane as you go. When you have cut all the way around, trim off any other bits of white pith you can see. Take the fruit in one hand and cut along one side of each each segment. You can then either cut down the other side to release the segment or you can carefully scrape the flesh in one movement from the centre to the edge – this will ensure you remove every bit of flesh from that side. Working over a bowl to catch any juice, cut each segment in half and set aside. Squeeze out the peel and membranes into the juice.

continued...

Next make the tiger's milk. Put the ginger and garlic in a small bowl with the coriander (cilantro) stems, lime juice, chilli and thyme. Add the reserved juice and leave for 5 minutes to infuse. Strain, then add a generous pinch of salt.

Put some iced water in a small bowl with a teaspoon of salt added. Add the red onion and leave to soak for 5 minutes. Drain and dry.

To prepare the sea bass, place it skin side down, then cut thin slices diagonally across the grain so you end up with fairly flat, skinless slices, similar to the way you would cut smoked salmon. Cut these in half. Alternatively, you can simply cut into thick strips, but I think the slices look prettier on the plate. Put in a bowl, sprinkle with a generous pinch of salt, and mix. After 2 minutes, add the tiger's milk and leave for a further 2 minutes only (it will carry on "cooking" after being removed).

Remove the sea bass from its marinade and arrange flat on a plate. Add the red onion slices, orange segments and tomatoes, then sprinkle with the coriander (cilantro) and basil. Serve immediately, with shots of the leftover marinade on the side if you like.

Note on fish

I prefer clean-tasting sea bass or bream for ceviche, but use whatever is freshest on the day. Just don't use anything that is liable to flake, and bear in mind that any firmer fish will need to marinate for a little longer.

COCONUT, LIME AND LEMONGRASS CHICKEN SALAD

Serves 4

For the chicken

1 tbsp coconut oil

6 boneless chicken thighs
  or 4 breasts, skin on

4 garlic cloves, finely sliced

2 thin slices of fresh
  root ginger, peeled and
  chopped

3 lemongrass stalks, outer
  leaves discarded, finely
  chopped

1 x 400ml tin/1¾ cups
  coconut milk

Finely grated zest and juice
  of 2 limes

2 Makrut lime leaves,
  shredded (optional)

1 tbsp fish sauce

Sea salt and crushed white
  peppercorns

Handfuls of mint,
  coriander (cilantro) and
  basil, to serve

continued...

In keeping with many Thai dishes, the citrus notes in this salad are sweet and fragrant, with most of the bite coming from the ginger and chilli.

First prepare the chicken. Heat the coconut oil in a large, shallow pan and add the chicken, skin side down. Fry on a medium to high heat until the skin is crisp and brown, then turn over. Add the garlic, ginger and lemongrass, then pour the coconut milk around the chicken. Add the lime zest and juice, the lime leaves, if using, and the peppercorns, and season with the fish sauce and some salt. Reduce the heat and leave to simmer, uncovered so the sauce reduces, until the chicken is cooked through, around 15 minutes. Remove the chicken. Strain the sauce and reserve.

continued...

For the salad

2 tbsp vegetable oil

2 shallots, finely sliced

1 large carrot, peeled and
  julienned

1 large courgette
  (zucchini), julienned

100g/1⅓ cups cauliflower
  florets, finely sliced

A small bunch of radishes,
  finely sliced

A bunch of spring onions
  (scallions), finely sliced
  on the diagonal

For the dressing

A small piece of fresh root
  ginger, peeled and grated

1 red chilli, finely chopped

Finely grated zest and juice
  of 1 lime

1 tbsp fish sauce

To assemble the salad, heat the vegetable oil in a small
pan and fry the shallots quite briskly until they are
translucent and well browned. Remove to drain on some
kitchen paper and set aside. Arrange the raw vegetables
over a large plate or platter. Slice or shred the chicken,
skin included, and add to the vegetables.

Whisk all the dressing ingredients together with
4 tablespoons of the reserved cooking sauce, and pour over
the salad. Sprinkle with the herbs and the fried shallots.

LEMON PIZZETTE

Makes 12 small or 8 large

For the dough

500g/3½–3⅔ cups strong white flour, plus extra for dusting

7g/¼oz instant dried yeast

10g/2 tsp salt

300ml/1¼ cups warm water

2 tbsp olive oil

For the meat topping

Fresh mozzarella, shredded

Very thinly sliced lemon

Italian fennel sausages, skinned

Dried chilli flakes (red pepper flakes)

Fresh basil leaves

Olive oil

Vegetarian variation

Substitute the fennel sausages for thinly sliced artichoke hearts.

The lemon and fennel combination here is one that appears frequently throughout this book, in both savoury and sweet dishes – they work so well together. Fennel is also wonderful with orange, so you can substitute if you like.

It doesn't make sense to make a smaller amount of dough, but you can freeze any you don't use – just wrap it into individual portions after it has risen and place in the freezer. Transfer to the refrigerator the night before you want to use it (or in the morning, for evening use) so it can defrost slowly, then proceed as normal.

To make the dough, mix the flour and yeast together in a large bowl, then add the salt. Gradually add the water and olive oil until you have a dough, then turn out onto a floured surface and knead until the dough is soft, smooth and elastic. (Alternatively, put the whole lot in a stand mixer and mix and knead with the dough hook.) Return to the bowl, cover with a damp tea towel or plastic wrap and leave until it has doubled in size.

For small pizzette (around 20cm/8-in diameter) divide the dough into 12 balls. For larger, 30cm/12-in pizzette, divide into 8. (Freeze any dough you are not using at this stage.)

Preheat your oven to its highest temperature. Preheat a pizza stone or baking tray/s.

Roll out each piece of dough to the desired size, pulling it out until it stops springing back. Add some shredded mozzarella. Blanch the lemon slices (allowing for a couple per pizzetta) in boiling water for 1 minute, then drain and cut into quarters. Arrange over the mozzarella, then crumble over the fennel sausages. Sprinkle over a few chilli flakes (red pepper flakes) and basil leaves, then drizzle with olive oil.

Transfer the pizzette to the preheated stone or baking trays, working in batches if necessary, and bake for 6–8 minutes. Serve immediately, sprinkled with extra basil leaves.

BLOOD ORANGE, BURRATA AND FREEKEH SALAD

Serves 4

100g/⅔ cup freekeh

600ml/2½ cups chicken or vegetable stock

2 garlic cloves, finely chopped

1 tsp finely grated bergamot zest (or lemon zest)

Juice of ½ bergamot (or lemon)

1 tbsp olive oil, plus extra for drizzling

2 small red onions, sliced vertically into thin wedges

A large bunch of chard, shredded

50ml/3½ tbsp water

2 large blood or blush oranges, peeled and sliced, any juice squeezed from the peel reserved

1 large or 2 small burrata

A handful of mint leaves

Sea salt and freshly ground black pepper

This is a very happy confluence of ingredients; smoky nuttiness from the freekeh, earthiness from the chard, a creamy sweetness from the burrata, all pulled together by the fragrant, sweet-sour citrus. The bergamot is purely optional as its flavour is subtle here, but if you can, please do: bergamots are still in season (just) when blood oranges come in, so it should be possible to find them. Use lemon zest instead if not.

First cook the freekeh. Soak it in plenty of cold water for 5 minutes, then drain and rinse thoroughly. Put in a medium saucepan with the stock, garlic and zest. Season with salt, then bring to the boil and leave to simmer for 15–20 minutes until cooked – it should be plumped up but still with some bite. Add the bergamot juice and leave to stand for a few minutes before straining.

Heat the olive oil in a large frying pan. Add the onion wedges and sauté over a medium heat until starting to turn translucent – you want them softened but not completely collapsed. Add the chard, along with the water, and cook over a gentle heat until the chard has wilted down and the stems are still al dente. Season with salt and pepper.

Arrange the freekeh over a large platter and top with the onions and chard. Pour over any reserved juice from the blood oranges – there should be a fair bit. Break up the burrata over the salad, then top with the orange slices and mint leaves. Drizzle over a little olive oil.

MARINATED SQUID, SMOKED CHILLI, FENNEL AND LEMON SALAD

Serves 4

60ml/¼ cup olive oil

Finely grated zest and juice of 1 lemon

1 tsp ouzo (optional)

Pinch of caster (superfine) sugar

½–1 tsp smoked chilli powder or paste (such as chipotle)

400g/14oz squid, cleaned and cut into rings, tentacles included

2 garlic cloves, finely chopped

200g/7oz new potatoes, boiled in their skins, kept warm then sliced (optional)

1 fennel bulb, finely sliced

1 lemon, segmented (see instructions on page 14), or use orange if you prefer

2 red chillies, finely sliced (deseeded for less heat if you like)

Leaves from small bunches of parsley, Greek basil (the small-leaved stuff if you can get it, otherwise regular basil) and oregano

Sea salt and freshly ground black pepper

There are two ways to cook squid quickly. The methods with which most people are familiar involve grilling and frying, which have to be done last minute. The advantage of the method in this recipe is all in the timing – you can blanch the squid, then leave it in its marinade until you need to serve it. This makes it the perfect, prepare-ahead salad. Just make sure that if you leave it to marinate in the refrigerator, you give it enough time to return to room temperature before you serve it.

In a large bowl, whisk together the olive oil, lemon zest and juice, ouzo, if using, sugar and chilli powder or paste. Add salt and pepper to taste.

Bring a large saucepan of salted water to the boil. When it is nicely rolling, add all the squid and garlic and boil for precisely 40 seconds. Drain and immediately add to the prepared marinade.

Leave the squid to marinate for at least an hour, then mix with the new potatoes, if using, fennel and lemon. Add the chillies, parsley, basil and oregano and toss everything gently together. Serve at room temperature.

BEEF CARPACCIO SALAD WITH
LEMON-MANDARIN-KOSHO DRESSING

Serves 4

500g/1lb 2oz piece of beef
fillet

A handful of lamb's lettuce
leaves

A handful of watercress or
landcress leaves

A few radishes

A few black sesame seeds

1 orange, diced

**For the carpaccio
dressing**

2 egg yolks

1–2 tsp lemon-mandarin-
kosho (see page 105),
to taste

2 tbsp orange juice

1 tbsp lemon juice

A pinch of sugar

75–100ml/5–7 tbsp
olive oil

Sea salt and freshly ground
black pepper

For the salad dressing

½ tsp sesame oil

1 red chilli, finely chopped

1 tbsp orange juice

1 tsp white wine vinegar

½ tsp runny honey

**A beef carpaccio will usually have a dressing similar to
a thin mayonnaise. This follows that tradition, but adds
the kosho, which really helps to ramp up the savoury
qualities of the dish. If you don't have any kosho made
up, you can add some very finely chopped preserved
citrus and fresh chilli to the dressing instead. You can use
mandarin juice in place of the orange juice, if you like.**

First prepare the beef for slicing. Wrap it tightly in plastic
wrap and put in the freezer for at least 30 minutes,
preferably a little longer (up to an hour), to firm it up.

Meanwhile, make the dressings. For the carpaccio
dressing, put the egg yolks, kosho and juices in a bowl and
whisk together with the sugar. Gradually drizzle in the oil,
initially a few drops at a time, until you have a fairly thin
emulsion. You may not need to use all the oil. Taste for
seasoning and add salt, pepper or more sugar if you think it
needs it. Set aside.

Whisk together the salad dressing ingredients and season
with salt and pepper. Set to one side.

Prepare the beef. Remove the plastic wrap, then using
your sharpest knife, slice as thinly as you can. Arrange over
4 serving plates and drizzle with the carpaccio dressing,
making sure you reserve some of it.

Put all the salad leaves in a bowl and drizzle over the salad
dressing. Mix then put a small pile of leaves on top of the
carpaccio, then finely chop the radish and add, along with
the orange. Sprinkle with sesame seeds.

JERUSALEM ARTICHOKE AND PRESERVED ORANGE SALAD

Serves 6–8 as a side or part of a mezze

juice of ½ lemon

8 medium artichokes

1 tbsp preserved Seville orange zest (see page 100)

2 tsp preserving liquor (see page 100)

Olive oil, for drizzling

A handful of micro coriander (cilantro) (optional)

I had no idea Jerusalem artichokes could be eaten raw until I was once served a salad of them by Danish cook Trine Hahnemann. They are a revelation: sweet and crisp – a bit like *jicama* but slightly denser in texture.

Add the juice from the lemon to a bowl of ice-cold water. Peel about the artichokes then slice them in very thin rounds, dropping them into the acidulated water as you go. When you are ready to serve, drain them thoroughly and arrange over a plate. Julienne the preserved Seville orange zest (see page 100) and mix with the liquor from the preserved orange, then thin with the fresh orange juice. Drizzle over the artichokes, followed by a drizzle of olive oil. This looks beautifully pure as it is, but is also good with a light sprinkling of micro coriander (cilantro).

MAIN COURSES

WHOLE BAKED FISH
WITH LEMON AND OUZO

Serves 4

1kg/2lb 3oz new potatoes,
scrubbed

2 tbsp olive oil, plus extra
for the fish and capers

30g/2 tbsp butter

Finely grated zest and
juice of 1 lemon, plus
1 lemon, sliced

1 head of garlic, broken up
into cloves, left unpeeled

1 large sea bass or similar
(around 1kg/2lb 3oz) or
2 smaller, cleaned
and descaled

A few sprigs of thyme and
or/lemon thyme and dill

100ml/7 tbsp white wine

50ml/3½ tbsp ouzo or
other anise-based spirit

2 tbsp capers

Sea salt and freshly ground
black pepper

continued...

**This is one of the easiest ways to cook fish. It is also a
complete, one-pot dish, although you can bake the fish
separately, wrapped in foil, if you prefer. I normally
make this with lemon, but it is also good with fragrant
mandarins, which work well with aniseedy ouzo.**

Preheat the oven to 200°C/400°F/Gas mark 6.

Boil the potatoes for 10 minutes in plenty of salted water
until just tender. Run under cold water until cool enough to
handle. Squash in your hands so they break roughly in half,
then put in a roasting tin.

Heat the olive oil and the butter together until the butter
has melted then add the lemon zest and juice. Pour all but a
tablespoon of this mixture over the potatoes and season with
salt and pepper. Add the garlic cloves, reserving a couple for
the fish. Roast in the oven for 30 minutes.

Cut a few slits into the fish on both sides. Peel and finely
slice the reserved garlic and stuff some into the slits along
with a few herb sprigs. Put the lemon slices, more herbs and
a few more slices of garlic in the cavity of the fish.

Put the fish on top of the potatoes, then drizzle over the
reserved tablespoon of lemony butter and a little more olive
oil. Mix the wine and ouzo together and pour this over the
fish and potatoes. Roast in the oven for a further 25–30
minutes until the fish is just cooked through.

continued...

For the lemon and ouzo sauce

2 egg yolks

1 tsp Dijon mustard

200ml/generous ¾ cup neutral-tasting oil, such as sunflower or groundnut

50ml/3½ tbsp Greek yogurt

2 tbsp ouzo or similar anise-based spirit

Juice of ½ lemon

A pinch of sugar (optional)

1 tbsp finely chopped dill

½ tsp fennel seeds, finely crushed (optional)

Meanwhile, make the sauce. Put the egg yolks and mustard in a bowl with a pinch of salt. Start drizzling in the oil, very gradually, whisking with a balloon whisk until it emulsifies and starts to thicken. At this point you can speed up the drizzling a little. When you have incorporated all the oil, whisk in the yogurt, ouzo and lemon juice. Season with salt, then taste – you may need a little more, along with a pinch of sugar to balance out the flavours. Stir in the dill and the fennel seeds, if using.

For the caper garnish, heat a tablespoon of olive oil in a frying pan. When very hot, add the capers – they will splutter for a few moments. When it subsides, remove from the heat. Pour over the fish and serve immediately.

TONKATSU WITH YUZU COLESLAW AND PONZU

Serves 4

For the pork

8 pork medallions or steaks, trimmed of fat

2 tbsp plain (all-purpose) flour

2 eggs, beaten

100g/2⅓ cups panko breadcrumbs

30g/2 tbsp butter, melted, or olive oil

Sea salt and black pepper

For the coleslaw

½ small green (pointed) cabbage

1 carrot, peeled and julienned

4 spring onions (scallions), finely chopped

½ tsp salt

½ tsp caster (superfine) sugar

2 tsp white wine vinegar

1 crisp apple, peeled and grated

continued...

Tonkatsu is the Japanese version of schnitzel, made with panko crumbs. You could serve it as such with lots of freshly squeezed lemon and it would still be a wonderful meal. But this is even better. Usually just juice is used in ponzu, but I do like to ramp up the flavour of the yuzu by adding powdered zest as well – that is where most of the fragrance is to be found.

First make the coleslaw. Shred the cabbage as finely as you can, then put in a colander with the carrot and spring onions (scallions). Sprinkle over the salt, sugar and vinegar, then leave to stand over a bowl or in the sink for an hour – this will have the effect of ridding the vegetables of any excess water and will prevent it from diluting the dressing later. Transfer the vegetables to a bowl and add the apple. Whisk together the mayonnaise, crème fraîche, yuzu juice, soy and powdered zest, if using. Pour over the vegetables and mix thoroughly. Sprinkle over the sesame seeds.

To make the tonkatsu, preheat the oven to 200°C/400°F/ Gas mark 6. Put the pork between sheets of plastic wrap and bash with a mallet or rolling pin until they are as thin as you can get without them breaking up. Put the flour on a plate and season with salt and pepper. Put the beaten eggs into a small bowl and the breadcrumbs on a separate plate. Dust each escalope with the seasoned flour, then pat off any excess before dropping into the egg wash and then the breadcrumbs. Arrange on a baking tray. Drizzle over the melted butter or oil and bake in the oven for around 10–12 minutes, by which point the pork should be cooked through and the breadcrumbs lightly browned.

continued...

1 tbsp mayonnaise

1 tbsp crème fraîche

1 tbsp yuzu juice, or more
to taste

A dash of dark soy sauce

½ tsp powdered yuzu zest
(optional)

1 tbsp sesame seeds

For the ponzu

3 tbsp dark soy sauce

1 tbsp mirin

1 tbsp rice vinegar

½ tsp sugar

1 thin slice of fresh root
ginger, peeled and finely
chopped

Juice of 1 mandarin

2 tbsp yuzu juice

1 tsp powdered yuzu zest

To make the ponzu, put the soy sauce, mirin, rice vinegar, sugar, ginger, mandarin juice and lime juice in a small saucepan. Simmer, stirring, until the sugar has dissolved, then immediately remove from the heat. Whisk in the yuzu juice and zest and strain into a small dipping sauce bowl.

Serve the pork with the coleslaw on the side and the ponzu for dipping.

SPICED SEA BASS WITH CITRUS BUTTER SAUCE

Serves 4

4 sea bass fillets, skin on

1 tbsp olive oil

30g/2 tbsp butter

2 garlic cloves, finely chopped

Finely grated zest and juice of 2 lemons

Juice of 1 large orange

100ml/7 tbsp water

Sea salt and freshly ground black pepper

For the rub

1 tsp flaky sea salt, pounded

½ tsp ground cardamom

¼ tsp ground cinnamon

¼ tsp ground ginger

¼ tsp ground white pepper

¼ tsp garlic powder

¼ tsp ground turmeric

To serve

350g/12oz spring greens, very finely shredded

350g/2½ cups cooked chickpeas (garbanzo beans)

The spicing here is fragrant rather than hot and has a vaguely Middle Eastern feel to it, so you could simply serve it with rice or couscous instead of the chickpeas and greens if you prefer.

Blot the sea bass fillets and lie skin-side down on kitchen paper. Combine all the rub ingredients and sprinkle evenly over the fillets. Press lightly.

Before you start frying the fish, cook the spring greens. Wash thoroughly, then put in a large lidded saucepan without shaking off too much water. Cover and heat gently until the greens have wilted down and are just al dente – they should be a fresh, bright green.

Heat the olive oil in a large frying pan. When hot, add the sea bass fillets, skin side down, and fry for a couple of minutes. Flip over and cook for a further 30 seconds. Remove from the frying pan and keep warm.

Add the butter, garlic, lemon zest and juice and orange juice to the pan. Turn up the heat and let the mixture bubble until you have a glossy, syrupy sauce. Pour into a jug.

Deglaze the pan with the water. Add the chickpeas and spring greens and stir to pick up any flavour residue. Season with salt and pepper.

Serve the fish with the chickpeas and greens, and the sauce spooned over.

MANDARIN CHICKEN WITH GIANT COUSCOUS AND CHARRED BROCCOLI

Serves 4

2 onions

2 tbsp olive oil

8–10 chicken thighs, bone in and skin on

Finely grated zest and juice of 3 mandarins

Finely grated zest and juice of 1 lime or ½ lemon

2 garlic cloves, finely chopped

A few sprigs of thyme or rosemary

100ml/7 tbsp vermouth

Sea salt and freshly ground black pepper

For the couscous

1 head of broccoli, cut into small florets, rinsed and drained

2 tbsp olive oil

Finely grated zest of 1 lemon

1 red chilli, finely chopped

200g/1⅓ cups giant couscous

500ml/2 cups plus 1 tbsp water or chicken stock

50g/⅔ cup flaked (slivered) almonds, lightly toasted

A family favourite, and easy enough for a simple midweek supper. If you can start marinating the chicken first thing in the morning, ready to cook at night, that is ideal; otherwise just a few minutes while the onions are cooking will be enough to help the flavours along.

Preheat the oven to 200°C/400°F/Gas mark 6. Peel and cut the onions into thin edges, then put in the base of a roasting tin and drizzle over a tablespoon of the olive oil. Add a splash of water to the tin and roast in the oven for 10 minutes.

Put the chicken thighs in a bowl and season well with salt and pepper. Rub in the mandarin and lime or lemon zests.

Remove the tin from the oven and give the onions a good stir – they should be well on their way to softening with very little colour. Sprinkle over the garlic, making sure most of it falls in the centre of the tin, then add the thyme or rosemary.

Arrange the chicken thighs over the onions. Whisk the vermouth with the citrus juices then pour this around the chicken. Drizzle over the remaining olive oil. Roast in the oven for 45 minutes, until the chicken is cooked through with a crisp golden skin and the liquid is syrupy.

Meanwhile, make the couscous. Toss the broccoli florets with a tablespoon of the oil. Arrange on a baking tray and sprinkle with salt, the lemon zest and chilli. Put in the oven, below the chicken, preferably with some space in between the two, and roast for 20 minutes. Remove from the oven – it should be lightly charred.

continued...

To cook the couscous, heat the remaining olive oil in a saucepan. Add the couscous and toast for a few minutes. Pour in the water or stock and cook gently, stirring, until all the liquid is absorbed and the couscous is soft, about 15 minutes. Check regularly and add a little more liquid if necessary towards the end if the couscous isn't yet done.

Toss the couscous with the broccoli and the almonds. Serve with the chicken, with the citrusy sauce and onions spooned over.

Variation

You don't have to make this with giant couscous – a quick couscous, rice or some potatoes would be just as good.

MARINATED CHICKEN WITH CHARRED LIMES, SAFFRON BUTTER AND SOFT FLATBREADS

Serves 4

1 chicken (or 2 poussin), each cut into 10 pieces, skin on

A large pinch of saffron strands

1 tbsp boiling water

100g/scant ½ cup butter

1 garlic clove, crushed

Sea salt and freshly ground black pepper

For the marinade

A large pinch of saffron strands

1 tbsp boiling water

250ml/generous 1 cup lime juice (or sour orange or lemon)

1 onion, coarsely grated

continued...

Sally Butcher and her husband Jamshid kindly talked me through this recipe, which is a Middle Eastern classic. Poussin are skinned, cut up and left to sit in a bath of lime juice for 24 hours, before they are grilled or barbecued, basted all the while with saffron butter. Persians normally use a concentrated bottled juice for this, which is seriously sherbety and a bit of an acquired taste. Use this or a regular bottled sort – or if you can find a use for zest (there are plenty of ideas dotted around this book!) use around 12–15 large limes.

Put the chicken in a refrigerator-friendly receptacle. Season generously with salt and pepper. Using a pestle and mortar, grind the saffron for the marinade with a pinch of salt and mix with the boiling water. Add to the citrus juice and pour the lot over the chicken or poussins, along with the onion. Refrigerate and marinate overnight.

The next day, either get your barbecue ready or heat your oven to its highest temperature. Grind and soak the saffron in the boiling water, as before, and put it in a saucepan with the butter and garlic. Melt together.

continued...

For the cucumber and yogurt sauce

200ml/generous ¾ cup yogurt

A handful of mint leaves, finely chopped

½ cucumber, peeled, halved lengthways, deseeded, grated and drained

A pinch of sugar

For the lime-pickled red onions

1 large red onion, thinly sliced

100ml/7 tbsp lime juice

1 tsp salt

A few cracked peppercorns

To serve

4 limes, halved

Soft flatbreads

Flat-leaf parsley, chopped

Lime-pickled red onions (see above)

Drain and pat dry the chicken pieces then either arrange over your barbecue or a baking tray. Baste with the butter and cook for 10 minutes. Baste again, cook for a further 10 minutes, then repeat. By this time the chicken should be cooked through and nicely browned and blistered. Reheat any remaining butter.

Put the limes on the barbecue or on a griddle pan for a couple of minutes.

Mix the yogurt with the mint and grated cucumber, and season with salt and a pinch of sugar.

To make the lime-pickled red onions, put the onions in a bowl and pour over freshly boiled water to cover. Leave to stand for 20 seconds, then drain. In a small bowl, mix the lime juice with the salt. Pour over the onions, add the peppercorns and stir to combine. If serving straight away, leave to stand for at least 30 minutes. Otherwise, transfer to a sterilized jar and store in the refrigerator until needed.

To serve, warm through the flatbreads. Serve the chicken torn from the bone and piled into flatbreads with the yogurt, any leftover basting butter, parsley, pickled onions and squeezes of the charred limes.

GRILLED AUBERGINES WITH MOZZARELLA AND YUZUKOSHO

Serves 4

3 fat, round aubergines (eggplants), cut into 2cm/¾-in rounds

Olive oil, for brushing

250g/9oz mozzarella, thickly sliced and drained in a colander

Sea salt and freshly ground black pepper

For the dressing

1 tbsp yuzukosho, or other type of kosho (see pages 105–106)

1 tbsp yuzu juice or lemon juice

Finely grated zest and juice of 1 mandarin (optional)

A dash of light soy sauce

For the greens and lentils

1 tbsp oil

2 spring onions (scallions), sliced diagonally

1 garlic clove, finely chopped

200g/7oz chard, stems and leaves separated, both sliced

continued...

I'm venturing into the murky realms of fusion here. This is a combination I tried on a fridge forage and I loved it – the aubergines (eggplants) are smoky and squidgy, the mozzarella is creamy and the dressing has just the right amount of hot, sweet, saltiness to offset any richness. Also, if you use, for example, the lemon-mandarin combination for kosho as described on page 106, you are still – just – in the world of Mediterranean flavours. Don't use the best mozzarella here as it will ooze; a cheap one actually works better.

First, grill or bake the aubergine (eggplant) slices. If you have the time to grill them on a griddle, do so, as you get the best smoky flavour that way, otherwise you can put them under a medium grill or even bake in the oven at 200°C/400°F/Gas mark 6 for 20 minutes. Whichever way you do it, brush first with olive oil and sprinkle with salt. Cook until they are browned, with char lines if on a griddle, and beautifully tender within.

While the aubergines are grilling, whisk the dressing ingredients together and taste. Adjust by adding more of any of the ingredients until you get the flavour you like.

To finish the aubergines, put them all on a baking tray and lay the mozzarella on top. Put under a hot grill for as short a time as possible, so the mozzarella browns lightly but is still soft and not too rubbery.

continued...

100g/3½oz sprouting
broccoli, cut into
sections

100g/3½oz oriental
greens, sliced lengthways

50g/1¾oz mizuna or any
other mustardy greens

A handful of shiso leaves
(optional)

100g/⅔ cup cooked
green lentils (preferably
al dente)

A dash of light soy sauce
or tamari (optional)

Meanwhile, for the greens, put the oil in a wok and heat until shimmering. Add the spring onions (scallions), garlic, chard stems and sprouting broccoli and stir fry for 2–3 minutes, until the broccoli is almost cooked. Add the chard leaves and oriental greens with a splash of water (or stock) and cook for a further minute. Add the mizuna and shiso leaves, if using, and wilt in, then stir through the lentils just to warm them. Season with salt and pepper, and a dash of soy sauce or tamari if you like.

Serve the mozzarella topped aubergines with the dressing, alongside the greens and lentils in a separate bowl.

FISH TACOS

Serves 4

4 firm, thick white fish
fillets, skinned and cut
in half

Olive oil

Sea salt and freshly ground
black pepper

For the marinade

2 tbsp olive oil

Finely grated zest and juice
of 1 lime

Finely grated zest and juice
of 1 mandarin (optional)

1 tsp ground cumin

continued...

This looks like a lot of work, but really it takes minutes to make the salsas while the fish gets a brief marinating. If you can't find tomatillos, use green tomatoes or, failing that, just use red.

You can experiment with the flavours in the salsa – I like something quite tart against savoury fish and sweet avocado, so in place of grapefruit I might use blood orange or physalis.

First prepare the fish. In a bowl, whisk together the marinade ingredients, pour over the fish fillets and leave to marinate for at least an hour.

continued...

½ tsp chilli powder

1 tsp dried oregano

1 tsp garlic powder

1 tsp salt

For the tomatillo, grapefruit and chilli salsa

4 tomatillos, diced

½ red onion, diced

1 garlic clove

1 large pink or red grapefruit

1 red chilli

A pinch of ground cumin

Juice of 1 lime

1 tsp red wine vinegar

2 tbsp chopped coriander (cilantro)

For the avocado salsa

1 large avocado, diced

Finely grated zest and juice of 1 lime

2 tbsp coconut cream

2 tbsp chopped coriander (cilantro)

To serve

Fresh corn tortillas

Shredded lettuce

Meanwhile, make the salsas. For the tomatillo, grapefruit and chilli salsa, start by finely chopping the garlic and the chilli, then segment and dice the grapefruit (see page 14). Mix the ingredients for each salsa in 2 separate bowls and season well with salt and pepper. Leave to stand – these are best at room temperature. (You can purée the avocado if you like a crema – I prefer it chunky.)

Heat a frying pan until very hot, then add a little olive oil. Add the fish fillets and cook until they are almost completely done (i.e. the flesh will be turning opaque up the sides), then flip for another minute. Remove from the pan.

Pile the fillets onto the tortillas and top with shredded lettuce and the salsas.

DAL WITH LEMON
OR LIME CURRY

Serves 4

For the dal

1 tbsp coconut oil

1 onion, finely chopped

200g/7oz sweet potato or squash, finely diced

2 garlic cloves, finely chopped

2cm/¾-in piece of fresh root ginger, peeled and finely chopped

2 tbsp finely chopped coriander (cilantro) stems (save the leaves for serving)

1 tsp ground cardamom

1 tsp ground turmeric

½ tsp ground cumin

½ tsp ground coriander

¼ tsp ground cinnamon

A pinch of ground cloves

continued...

I love this combination, not least because compartmentalizing flavours as I've done here can be very useful when feeding a family – children not yet able to handle the hot and sour flavours of the lemon curry will be happy with the sweet and mild spices of the dal.

Giving the option of using lemons or limes for the curry pays lip service to the fact that very few people outside the US and the UK distinguish between them. Regardless, the results will be sour and you can make it as hot as you like.

Serve with basmati rice or with some paratha, with perhaps some lightly steamed greens on the side.

Heat the coconut oil in a large saucepan or flameproof casserole. Add the onion and sauté for several minutes until starting to soften. Add the sweet potato or squash, garlic and ginger, and cook for a few more minutes. Add the coriander (cilantro) stems and all the spices, then stir in the mung beans. Pour in the coconut milk and water, then bring to the boil. Season generously with salt and pepper. Simmer, covered, until the mung beans are tender, keeping an eye on it as you don't want it to get too dry. Before serving add the lemon or lime juice and sprinkle with coriander leaves.

continued...

300g/1½ cups mung beans (moong dal)

1 x 400ml tin/1¾ cups coconut milk

500ml/generous 2 cups water

Juice of 1 lemon or lime

Sea salt and freshly ground black pepper

Coriander (cilantro) leaves, to serve

For the lemon or lime curry

4 lemons or 6 limes

1 tbsp coconut oil

1 tsp cumin seeds

1 tsp mustard seeds

1 tsp coriander seeds

A few curry leaves

¼ fresh coconut, grated

1 large onion, finely chopped

5cm/2-in piece of fresh root ginger, peeled and grated

4 garlic cloves, crushed

1 tsp ground turmeric

2 tsp Kashmiri chilli powder

500ml/generous 2 cups water

1 tbsp jaggery or soft light brown sugar

Top and tail and lemons or limes, then cut (with peel) into 1cm/½-in dice. Put the lemons or limes in a saucepan and cover with water. Bring to the boil and simmer for 5 minutes. Drain thoroughly.

Melt the coconut oil in a saucepan or flameproof casserole. Add the whole spices with the curry leaves and fry until the mustard seeds start popping. Add the grated coconut and fry for a few minutes until it is looking lightly toasted, then add the onion, ginger and garlic. Continue to cook for a few minutes, then add the turmeric and chilli powder.

Add the lemons or limes along with the water and the jaggery. Simmer until the lemons or limes are tender and the sauce is well reduced – it should retain its light, bright yellow. Add a splash more water if you think it needs it.

LINGUINE WITH LEMON AND ASPARAGUS

Serves 4

250g/9oz linguine (or spaghetti at a pinch)

300g/10½oz asparagus, trimmed

Olive oil, for drizzling

30g/2 tbsp butter

Finely grated zest and juice of 1 large lemon

4 egg yolks

50g/1¾oz hard cheese, such as Parmesan or Pecorino

Sea salt and freshly ground black pepper

A very simple dish, reliant on good ingredients, so wait until early summer when asparagus is abundant and you can get large, sweet, fragrant lemons from Italy. I specify a "hard cheese" here – I would normally use Parmesan or Pecorino in this recipe, but if you are vegetarian it is now easy to find rennet-free alternatives.

Bring a large pot of water to the boil and salt generously. Add the linguine and cook until just al dente. Drain, reserving a small cupful of the cooking liquid.

Meanwhile, heat a griddle pan until it is as hot as you can get it – it should be too hot to hold your hand over comfortably. Wash the asparagus, shake off the excess liquid and put on the griddle. Drizzle with a little olive oil and grill for 3–4 minutes on each side. Remove and slice each spear in half on the diagonal.

Melt the butter in the pasta pan then add the lemon zest. Turn the heat down as low as you can, then whisk the lemon juice and egg yolks into the butter, until you have an emulsion. Add some of the reserved pasta liquid, a tablespoon at a time, until you have a sauce the texture of single (light) cream – it should be silky-smooth and just coat the pasta when you add it without being cloying. Add the pasta and asparagus to the pan and toss to coat in the sauce.

Serve with plenty of black pepper and the cheese shaved over the top.

ROAST VEGETABLES WITH FETA AND ORANGE

Serves 4

3 small red onions, peeled
and quartered

2 red (bell) peppers,
cut into strips

1 green (bell) pepper,
cut into strips

2 courgettes (zucchini),
cut into chunks on the
diagonal

200g/7oz piece of
pumpkin, cut into thin
wedges

1 head of garlic, cloves
separated, unpeeled

A handful of oregano
leaves, plus extra to serve

2 whole oranges plus
the juice of 2 medium
oranges

2 tbsp olive oil

75g/¾ cup black olives

400g/14oz feta, broken
into chunks

Sea salt and freshly ground
black pepper

Parsley leaves, to serve

I think this is substantial enough on its own, but you could add a side salad if you like, or some leftover grains of some sort.

I don't eat the skin of the oranges unless it is particularly thin, but somehow the orange does taste better roasted when left unpeeled.

Preheat the oven to 200°C/400°F/Gas mark 6.

Put all the vegetables into a large roasting tin and sprinkle in the garlic cloves and oregano. Top and tail the 2 whole oranges then cut into fairly thick slices. Cut each slice into quarters. Add all this orange to the roasting tin, then pour over the orange juice. Season with salt and pepper and drizzle everything with the olive oil.

Roast in the oven for 45 minutes, then turn everything over, gently. Sprinkle over the olives and dot the feta around. Roast for another 15 minutes. The feta should be soft and creamy and everything else should be on the verge of charring, but nicely soft on the bottom.

Serve immediately, sprinkled with oregano and parsley, direct from the tin, or you can remove everything to a serving platter and squish the garlic cloves into the tin juices to pour over.

SIDE
DISHES

FENNEL AND LEMON DAUPHINOISE

Serves 4

A slice of butter, plus extra for greasing

2 fennel bulbs

1 lemon

300ml/1¼ cups whipping (heavy) cream

50ml/3½ tbsp milk

1 tsp plain (all-purpose) flour

3 tbsp breadcrumbs

3 tbsp roughly grated Pecorino

A grating of nutmeg

Sea salt and freshly ground black pepper

The lemon in this recipe melds seamlessly with the fennel and cream despite being unpeeled – you will get the odd burst of sour, but it never feels *de trop*. This is a perfect side dish for any simply grilled fish or meat.

Preheat the oven to 180°C/350°F/Gas mark 4. Rub a gratin dish with butter. Bring 2 saucepans of water to the boil.

Trim off and reserve any leafy fronds from the fennel, then trim the base, removing the bare minimum as you want the fennel to hold together at the roots. Finely slice lengthways. Top and tail the lemon, then slice as finely as you can, preferably with a mandoline. Add the fennel and lemon to separate saucepans of boiling water and blanch – the fennel for 3–4 minutes, the lemon for 1 minute only. Drain both.

Arrange the fennel and lemon in the gratin dish, seasoning the layers with salt and pepper as you go. In a bowl, whisk the cream with the milk and flour (just to combine, you do not want it to thicken). Pour this mixture over the fennel and lemon.

Finely chop the reserved fennel fronds and mix with the breadcrumbs and cheese. Grate in some nutmeg (a few rasps will be enough), then stir and sprinkle over the gratin. Dice the butter and dot it over the gratin. Bake in the oven for around 1 hour until the fennel and lemon are tender and the top is crisp and golden brown.

CARAMELIZED POTATOES WITH ORANGE

Serves 4

1kg/2lb 3oz small new potatoes, scrubbed but unpeeled

100g/½ cup caster (superfine) sugar

75g/⅓ cup butter

Finely grated zest of ½ sour orange and juice of 2 sour oranges (or zest of ½ orange and ½ lime, juice of 1 orange and 1 lime)

Sea salt

The idea of caramelized potatoes is a Scandinavian one, but the addition of orange is all mine. Slathering potatoes in butter and sugar is clearly not something you want to do every day – the Scandinavians serve it as part of Christmas dinner – but is worth having as part of the repertoire to complement rich, earthy casseroles. I like to serve them with a red-wine beef or venison casserole flavoured with juniper.

It is traditional to peel the potatoes after boiling them and the caramel does stick to them better that way – but you can leave them unpeeled if you prefer; it won't make too much of a difference.

Put the potatoes in a saucepan and cover with water. Bring to the boil and add salt. Simmer until knife-tender, around 12–15 minutes. Drain and cool under running water, then peel them, if you like – you should find that the skins slip off very easily.

Melt the sugar in a large, heavy-based frying pan over a medium heat. Leave it alone, perhaps just giving it a shake every so often, until it has caramelized – it will start around the edges and eventually turn a light golden brown. Add the butter (be careful, it may splutter) and allow it to melt into the caramel, keeping the stirring to a minimum. Whisk in the zest, juice and a pinch of salt. Add the potatoes then leave to cook, slowly, and turning regularly, until the caramel has reduced down and the potatoes are well coated.

CHICORY BRAISED WITH GRAPEFRUIT, MANDARIN AND SOY

Serves 4

1 tbsp olive oil

1 tbsp runny honey

4 heads of chicory (endive), cut in half lengthways

50g/3½ tbsp butter

Finely grated zest of 1 mandarin and 50ml/3½ tbsp juice

1 tsp finely grated grapefruit zest and 50ml/3½ tbsp juice

30ml/2 tbsp dark soy sauce

A few sprigs of thyme

Sea salt and freshly ground black pepper

This dish is heaven for anyone who loves bitter flavours – it is layering bitter on bitter, but it is slightly tempered with the mandarin juice, honey and butter. I confess I can easily eat the lot in one sitting.

It is best served alongside some grilled meat – perhaps a fatty pork steak or a thick slice of gammon. Or eat it as a supper dish with some mashed potato or bread for mopping.

Heat the olive oil in a large frying pan. Melt the honey in a small saucepan then brush over the cut edges of the chicory (endive). Sear the chicory in the frying pan, cut side down, until it has started to caramelize, then flip over and cook for a couple more minutes. Add the butter, citrus zests and juices and the soy sauce, pouring them around the chicory, then sprinkle in the thyme sprigs and season with salt and pepper. Simmer, turning regularly, until the chicory is glossy and tender, and the liquids have reduced to a syrup.

ROAST TOMATOES WITH LEMON AND LEMON THYME

Serves 4

400g/14oz small to
  medium vine tomatoes
1 tbsp olive oil
1 large lemon

To serve

Lemon thyme
Shredded basil (optional)
Capers (optional)
Sea salt

I can't remember what led me to this idea, but I'm so glad I tried it. I had always been a bit either/or with tomatoes and lemons but this is a revelation – the lemon sweetens and caramelizes in a very different way from the tomatoes and they complement one another perfectly. These are wonderful with grilled fish or steak, or just folded through some pasta.

Separate the tomatoes from the vine but leave the core leaves. Heat a heavy-based frying pan to as hot as you can get it. Add the olive oil and the tomatoes. Cook, shaking regularly, until the tomatoes are threatening – but not quite ready – to burst out of their skins. This won't take long. Cut the peel off the lemon (see instructions on page 14) and dice the flesh, taking out any pips as you go. Add this into the pan – it should sizzle and start caramelizing almost immediately. Shake a couple of times and remove. Serve sprinkled with the salt and lemon thyme, and the shredded basil, if you like. Capers are also a good addition here; you can add them just before the lemon so they can sizzle for a moment on their own first.

ROASTED CAULIFLOWER WITH LEMON, NIGELLA SEEDS AND GREMOLATA

Serves 4

1 large cauliflower

1 head of garlic

1 tbsp olive oil

Finely grated zest and
  juice of 1 lemon or lime
  (reserve the zest for the
  gremolata, below)

1 tsp nigella seeds

½ tsp cumin seeds

½ tsp dried chilli flakes
  (red pepper flakes) or
  a finely chopped fresh
  chilli

Sea salt

For the gremolata

2 garlic cloves

Small bunch of coriander
  (cilantro)

Finely grated zest of 1
  lemon or lime (above)

Sea salt

Gremolata is a very useful thing to know how to make quickly as most people will usually have some kind of citrus zest, garlic and soft herb in the house. I use coriander (cilantro) here as this recipe has Asian notes to it, but it is more traditional to use parsley. You can also use preserved citrus instead of fresh zest. You can sprinkle this gremolata over any meaty casserole, or turn into a dressing for grilled chicken or fish, as suggested below.

Preheat the oven to 200°C/400°F/Gas mark 6. Break the cauliflower into florets and cut the larger florets in half lengthways. Break up the head of garlic and leave the cloves unpeeled. Add both to a roasting tin. Mix together the olive oil with the juice of the lemon or lime (reserve the finely grated zest). Add the salt, nigella seeds, cumin seeds and dried chilli flakes (red pepper flakes), or you can use a finely chopped fresh chilli instead if you prefer. Pour this over the cauliflower and garlic, turn to coat then spread out into an even layer. Roast for around 35–40 minutes until the cauliflower is nicely charred and al dente.

To make the gremolata, finely chop the garlic cloves and the coriander (cilantro). Mix together with the reserved lemon or lime zest and season with salt. This can also be turned into a type of dressing with more olive oil and citrus juice if you prefer. Serve separately at the table.

SOMETHING SWEET

BLOOD ORANGE AND RHUBARB MERINGUE PIE

Serves 6

For the pastry

225g/1¾ cups plain (all-purpose) flour, plus extra for dusting

150g/⅔ cup butter, chilled and diced

1 egg yolk

A pinch of salt

For the filling

400g/14oz rhubarb, preferably the pink forced kind, cut into short (2cm/¾-in) lengths

60g/⅓ cup caster (superfine) sugar

Finely grated zest of 2 blood oranges and juice of up to 4 blood oranges

1 tbsp cornflour (cornstarch)

3 egg yolks

30g/1 tbsp butter (optional)

continued...

Most meringue pies use a sweet pastry, but as I find the meringue so sweet, I think it is better served with a very buttery shortcrust (pie dough), so I take out the sugar. The butter in the filling is optional – it's not always used and I think it adds a richness, making the filling more like curd and less like custard.

First make the pastry. Either whiz the flour and butter in a food processor or rub in by hand until the mixture resembles fine breadcrumbs, then add the egg yolk and salt. Mix briefly, adding a little chilled water if necessary, until you can bring the pastry together into a ball – it should need no more than a tablespoon. Wrap in plastic wrap and chill for at least 30 minutes in the refrigerator. Preheat the oven to 190°C/375°F/Gas mark 5.

Roll out the pastry on a lightly floured work surface and use to line a pie dish (between 21 and 23cm/8¼ and 9-in diameter). Prick all over with a fork, then line with baking parchment and fill with baking beans. Bake for 20 minutes, then remove the beans and bake for a further 5 minutes or so until the pastry is a light golden brown. Remove from the oven.

To make the filling, put the rhubarb into a baking dish, sprinkle with the sugar and orange zest and roast in the oven for 30–35 minutes, stirring every so often – if you are organized you can cook this at the same time as you are blind baking the pastry. Strain the rhubarb juice into a measuring jug and set aside the solids. Add enough blood orange juice to make up the rhubarb juice to 250ml/1 cup plus 1 tbsp. Use a small amount of the liquid to whisk the cornflour (cornstarch) into a thin paste in a bowl, and heat the rest in a medium saucepan.

continued...

For the meringue topping

4 egg whites (left from pastry and filling)

225g/1¼ cups caster (superfine) sugar

½ tsp cream of tartar

When the liquid is hot, pour some of it over the cornflour mixture, whisking constantly, then pour this back into the saucepan. Stir over a low heat until the mixture thickens – this is likely to happen very suddenly. Add the egg yolks and butter, if using, and continue to whisk. Remove from the heat and stir through the reserved rhubarb. Pour into the cooked pastry case. If you have time, leave it to cool and chill down completely as it will help the texture enormously and prevent possible separation.

To make the meringue, whisk the egg whites in a large bowl until well aerated and just starting to form stiff peaks. Continuing to whisk, add the sugar a tablespoon at a time until the meringue is beautifully stiff and glossy, then add the remaining sugar all at once, and sprinkle in the cream of tartar. Pipe or pile the meringue over the filling.

Bake in the oven for around 15–20 minutes until the meringue is a dappled golden brown. I love this both hot and cold and I don't think it needs any embellishment.

BLACKBERRY, ORANGE AND ORANGE BLOSSOM CLAFOUTIS

Serves 4–6

For the dried citrus zest

Pared zest of 2 oranges (this will make more than the recipe calls for – store the remainder in an airtight container or mix with sugar)

For the baking dish

30g/2 tbsp butter, softened

2 tsp dried orange zest (above), ground to a powder

2 tbsp demerara sugar

For the blackberries

300g/2¼ cups blackberries

2 tbsp caster (superfine) sugar

2 tbsp crème de mûre

For the batter

50g/6 tbsp plain (all-purpose) flour

50g/¼ cup caster (superfine) sugar

A pinch of salt

continued...

Two of my favourite aromas – blackberries cooking and orange blossom – make this quite a blissful dessert for me. If you can get Mandarine Napoléon, please use it instead of an orange liqueur as it is so, so much nicer.

To make the dried orange zest, simply put your pared zest on a wire rack and toast in the oven (on its lowest setting, if above 100°C/200°F, with the door slightly ajar) for anything between 30 minutes and 3 hours, until parchment-dry. Try to avoid letting them brown too much as you don't want them to taste burnt – the original colour should be preserved as much as possible. If you have space and time, arrange on a rack again and leave somewhere warm and dry, for example in an airing cupboard, near a radiator or on a sunny windowsill. The best way to store dried citrus is in an airtight container, somewhere cool and dark.

Put the blackberries in a bowl and sprinkle over the sugar and crème de mûre. Leave to stand for an hour.

Preheat the oven to 180°C/350°F/Gas mark 4. Spread the butter over the base of a shallow ovenproof dish (between 21 and 23cm/8¼ and 9-in diameter). Mix the orange zest and demerara sugar together and sprinkle this over the butter. Make sure the dish is evenly covered.

Put the flour in a mixing bowl with the caster (superfine) sugar and salt. Give a quick whisk to get rid of any lumps.

continued...

200ml/¾ cup plus 1 tbsp
  whole milk

50ml/3½ tbsp
  single cream

30g/1 tbsp butter, melted

1 tsp finely grated orange
  zest and juice of
  ½ orange

1 tsp orange blossom
  water

2 tsp Grand Marnier,
  or ideally Mandarine
  Napoléon (optional)

2 eggs

To serve

1 tbsp icing
  (confectioners') sugar

1 tsp dried orange zest,
  ground to a powder

Pouring cream

In a separate bowl, mix together the milk, cream, melted
butter, orange zest and juice, orange blossom water and
liqueur, if using. Make a well in the middle of the flour and
sugar, then break in the eggs. Using a whisk, work in the
flour, incorporating from the edge of the well, until you
have a thick paste, then gradually incorporate the wet
ingredients. (You can instead put everything in a food
processer and blend.)

Spoon the blackberries into the prepared dish, straining
them a little as you go, and making sure they are evenly
spread. Pour over the batter and bake in the oven for around
25–30 minutes until slightly puffed up and a light golden
brown – it should still be slightly wobbly in the middle.

Mix the icing (confectioners') sugar and orange zest together.
Let the clafoutis cool a little, then sprinkle over the sugar
and zest mixture. Serve with pouring cream.

SUSSEX POND PUDDINGS

Serves 8

25g/1½ tbsp butter, plus extra for greasing

200g/1½ cups self-raising (self-rising) flour, plus extra for dusting

A pinch of salt

75g/2½oz suet

About 150ml/10 tbsp milk

For the filling

150g/⅔ cup butter

150g/¾ cup demerara sugar

3 pieces of stem ginger, finely chopped

8 kumquats or limequats

Variation

If you would like to make the classic Sussex pond pudding, use the same amount of suet pastry to line a 2-litre/3½ pint basin. Use all the butter and sugar in the same way, omitting the stem ginger, and use 1 whole lemon, orange or perhaps a couple of limes, making sure you pierce them thoroughly all over with a skewer. Steam for 3½–4 hours.

This pudding is the exception to my rule that kumquats are only worth bothering with if candied, as they infuse beautifully with the sugar and butter in this recipe, which gives a similar effect. Suet puddings are celebrated by the British and viewed with suspicion by everyone else – I love them and have found them infinitely adaptable (see variation, below).

Incidentally, this quantity of suet pastry can be put to good use in other citrusy ways. Try rolling it out into a large rectangle and filling with marmalade for a roly poly.

Generously butter 8 individual-sized pudding basins and set aside. Put the flour and salt into a bowl, then rub in the suet and butter. Gradually add the milk, cutting it in with a knife until you have a fairly soft, but roll-able dough. Knead lightly to make sure it is well combined (it will not be very smooth because of the suet) and not sticky, then turn out onto a floured surface. Divide the mixture into 8 – the easiest way to do this is by weighing it and dividing accordingly. Roll each piece of dough into a round, then cut a quarter out of it. Use each larger piece of the circle to line the pudding basins.

Cut up the butter for the filling into small squares and divide half of it between the 8 basins. Follow with half the demerara sugar and stem ginger. Stand the kumquats or limequats upright in the centre of the butter and sugar. Cover with the rest of the butter, sugar and ginger. Form the remaining pieces of dough into rounds and use to cover the puddings, making sure you seal the edges together.

Cover each of the puddings with pleated foil and tie firmly around the rim – if you have a supply of rubber bands, these are the easiest thing to use. Steam for around 2 hours until golden brown. When you are ready to serve, turn out and serve with pouring cream or crème anglaise.

BLOOD ORANGE AND CARDAMOM TARTE TATIN

Serves 6

2–3 blood oranges, depending on size

30ml/2 tbsp water

100g/½ cup granulated sugar

75g/⅓ cup unsalted butter, chilled and diced

Seeds extracted from 2 tsp cardamom pods, lightly crushed

300g/10½oz block of puff pastry

Plain (all-purpose) flour, for dusting

For the crème anglaise

250ml/1 cup plus 1 tbsp whole milk

250ml/1 cup plus 1 tbsp double (heavy) cream

1 tsp cardamom pods, lightly crushed

1 coffee bean

3cm/1¼-in piece of vanilla pod

50g/¼ cup caster (superfine) sugar

6 egg yolks

A citrus spiced tarte Tatin is proper winter comfort food, best eaten in February when blood oranges are in season and we need that hit of spice and colour to see us through. There are elements to this dish that transfer very well to other types of desserts. For example, you can exchange pastry for a sponge batter to make an upside-down cake.

If you don't want to make crème anglaise you can serve instead with Chantilly cream – just whip cream until fairly stiff and stir in a tablespoon of icing (confectioners') sugar mixed with a generous pinch of finely ground cardamom.

Preheat the oven to 180°C/350°F/Gas mark 4.

Top and tail the blood oranges, then slice very thinly. Set aside.

Put the water in the base of a 23cm/9-in cast-iron skillet or similar ovenproof pan. Sprinkle the sugar over the water in an even layer. Heat gently, resisting the urge to stir, just shaking every so often, until the sugar has melted and turned a light golden brown – you don't want it too dark at this stage. The water will help stop it browning too quickly around the edges. Remove from the heat and stir in the butter and cardamom seeds, trying not to froth it up too much.

Arrange the best orange slices in the caramel. On a lightly floured work surface, thinly roll out the pastry (to around 3mm/⅛-in), then prick all over with a fork. Cut into a round very slightly larger than your skillet, then lie it over the oranges, making sure the edges are tucked in.

continued…

Bake in the oven for around 30 minutes until the pastry is golden brown.

For the crème anglaise, put the milk and cream in a saucepan with the cardamom pods, coffee bean, vanilla and 1 tablespoon of the sugar. Bring to the boil, slowly. When on the point of boiling, remove from the heat and leave to infuse until cool.

Meanwhile, whisk the egg yolks and remaining sugar together until pale with a mousse-like consistency. Reheat the milk and cream until almost at boiling point. Pour the milk over the egg yolks and sugar in a steady stream, stirring constantly, then rinse out the pan. Pour everything back into the pan and stir on a low heat until the custard thickens – it should be thick enough to coat the back of a spoon well enough that you can draw a line through it.

Strain the custard into a jug. Serve hot or cold, but make sure you cover with plastic wrap – touching the top layer of the custard – to stop a skin from forming.

ORANGE, PECAN AND CINNAMON ROLLS

Makes 12

For the dough

250ml/1 cup plus
1 tbsp milk

75g/⅓ cup butter

350g/2⅔ cups strong
white bread flour

150g/1 cup plus 2 tbsp
wholemeal (wholewheat)
spelt flour

10g/⅓oz instant
dried yeast

75g/⅓ cup soft light
brown sugar

A large pinch of salt

1 egg

Finely grated zest of 1
orange

Oil, for greasing

continued...

These are extremely satisfying to make, and even more
satisfying to pull apart and eat. I particularly love
that the rolls can push themselves up when I have
optimistically crammed them in a little too tightly – it
means you get slightly more surface area to glaze and a
little more caramelization.

Put the milk in a saucepan and bring up to almost boiling
point. Remove from the heat and add the butter. Leave to
stand until the butter has melted and it has cooled to blood
temperature.

Put the flours in a large bowl with the yeast, sugar and salt.
Make a well in the middle. Beat the egg into the milk and
butter mixture and stir in the orange zest. Add this to the
flour and stir until well combined – you will find that you
have a very soft, sticky dough.

Lightly oil your hands and the work surface, then turn
out the dough. Knead by sliding your fingers under the
dough, pulling it up, and slapping it back down onto the
work surface. When you move your hands up away from
the dough it will come with you – stretch it upwards and
to the sides at the same time, then tuck it back under when
you repeat the whole motion of lifting it again. After a few
minutes you will have a dough that is no longer sticky and
can be formed into a smooth ball.

Put the dough into an oiled bowl then cover with plastic
wrap or a damp cloth. Leave to rise for around 1½ hours.

continued...

For the filling

50g/⅓ cup raisins

50ml/3½ tbsp bourbon

100g/scant ½ cup butter,
  softened, plus extra
  for greasing

50ml/3½ tbsp
  maple syrup

25g/2 tbsp soft dark
  brown sugar

1 tsp ground cinnamon

1 tsp ground mixed spice

A pinch of salt

75g/¾ cup
  chopped pecans

50g/1¾oz finely chopped
  candied orange peel

To glaze

1 egg, beaten

1 tbsp orange marmalade

1 tbsp soft light brown
  sugar

1 tbsp bourbon or water

While the dough is rising, make the filling. Put the raisins and bourbon in a small saucepan and bring to the boil, then remove from the heat and leave to infuse. Beat the butter with the maple syrup, sugar, spices and salt until you have a creamy, toffee-coloured butter.

Preheat the oven to 200°C/400°F/Gas mark 6. Line a 25–26cm/10-in round, deep cake tin with baking parchment, and butter generously. Allow the parchment to stand proud of the tin (this will help when removing the cooked buns from the tin).

Turn the risen dough out and roll or pat out into a rectangle of around 30 x 23cm/12 x 9-in. It will spring back to start with, but persevere and it will eventually yield. Spread the butter mixture over the dough, then sprinkle with the raisins, pecans and candied zest. Roll up tightly, then cut into 12 rounds.

Arrange the rounds, cut sides up/down, in the prepared cake tin. Brush with the beaten egg, then leave for around another 30 minutes and brush again. Bake in the oven for 20–25 minutes until a rich golden brown and well risen.

Meanwhile, melt the marmalade and sugar together with the bourbon or water in a small saucepan. Brush over the buns when they come out of the oven, then remove from the tin en masse by lifting out the baking parchment. Leave to cool.

BERGAMOT AND ROSE
TURKISH DELIGHT PAVLOVA

Serves 6–8

For the pavlova base

6 large egg whites

300g/1⅔ cups caster (superfine) sugar

1 tsp cornflour (cornstarch)

1 tsp white wine vinegar

150g/5¼oz rose and bergamot Turkish delight, finely chopped

For the filling

500ml/generous 2 cups double (heavy) cream

25g/2¾ tbsp icing (confectioners') sugar

150g/5¼oz lemon or lemon and bergamot curd

1–2 tbsp limoncello

50g/1¾oz rose and bergamot Turkish delight, finely diced

A few crystallized or fresh rose petals, to decorate

You can make this into one, joyous, celebratory pavlova, or make individual meringues. It is of course endlessly adaptable – you can use any sort of Turkish delight or curd.

First make the meringue base – this can be made ahead of time and kept for several days in an airtight container, or frozen. Preheat the oven to 160°C/325°F/Gas mark 3. Draw a circle the size of a dinner plate on a piece of baking parchment, for guidance, and turn the parchment upside down.

Whisk the egg whites until they have reached the soft peak stage – airy and light, but not yet very stiff and dry. Start adding the sugar, a dessertspoon at a time, whisking vigorously, until all the sugar has been incorporated and the meringue is glossy and keeps its shape. Mix the cornflour (cornstarch) and vinegar together and incorporate this, then fold in the Turkish delight.

Spoon the meringue onto the baking parchment, staying within the marked circle. Make a slight dip in the centre if you like and make sure plenty of peaks form by lightly touching the meringue with the back of a spoon and pulling it away.

Put the meringue in the oven and turn the temperature down to 140°C/275°F/Gas mark 1. Leave to bake for between 1 and 1½ hours, then turn off the oven and leave in the oven until it has cooled down. The meringue should easily peel away from the paper.

To assemble, whisk the cream with the icing (confectioners') sugar until billowy – make sure it isn't too stiff. Stir through most of the lemon curd, the limoncello and the Turkish delight, but go easy – you want a rippled effect, not homogeneity. Top with more lemon curd, Turkish delight and the rose petals.

GIN AND BITTER GRAPEFRUIT GRANITA

**Makes about
750ml/1½ pints**

Finely grated zest and juice
of 1 grapefruit (yellow
or pink)

A few sprigs of mint
(grapefruit mint if
you have it, spearmint
otherwise)

125g/scant ⅔ cup
granulated sugar

250ml/generous
1 cup water

250ml/generous 1 cup
tonic water

50ml/3½ tbsp gin

Grapefruit bitters, to serve
(optional)

**This recipe makes a superbly refreshing granita, perfect
on a hot day, but also especially good as a palate cleanser.
You can use the recipe as a template for other citrus/
alcohol combinations. Try lime with ginger ale and rum,
with a dash of angostura or lemon with vodka.**

Put the grapefruit zest, mint and sugar into a saucepan with
the water. Stir over a gentle heat until the sugar has dissolved
then turn up the heat and bring to the boil. Remove from
the heat immediately, then add the tonic water, gin and
grapefruit juice. Leave to cool to room temperature, then
chill in the refrigerator.

Strain the liquid into a lidded freezer-proof box. You need
it to be fairly wide, so the granita is quite shallow, about
2–3cm/1-in deep. Freeze for an hour, or until a layer of ice
has formed around the edge of the granita. Scrape this off
with a fork and beat into the rest of the mixture. Repeat this
every 30 minutes, until you have a granita formed of ice
crystals. Leave in the freezer until you are ready to eat, but
if you are leaving it for any length of time, you are going to
need to break it up fairly regularly. Serve in small glasses,
with a dash of grapefruit bitters, if you like.

LEMON ICE CREAM WITH ALMOND AND FENNEL PRALINE

Makes about 800ml/1¾ pints

For the ice cream

Finely grated zest and juice of 3 lemons

150g/¾ cup granulated sugar

A pinch of salt

500ml/2 cups double (heavy) cream

For the almond and fennel seed praline

75g/½ cup blanched almonds, roughly chopped (you can also use flaked almonds)

1 tsp fennel seeds

A generous pinch of sea salt

150g/¾ cup granulated sugar

50ml/3½ tbsp water

This is the best method for a no-cook ice cream I've found, based loosely on one in the manual from my 20-year-old ice-cream maker. It is beautifully fresh tasting – sherbety, even – and much nicer than lemon sorbet.

I have also made this ice cream using a combination of lemon and orange, with a praline of pistachios and cardamom seeds. Well worth trying.

Put the lemon zest in a food processor with the sugar and salt. Blitz until the zest has all but vanished into the sugar – this will ensure you get a perfectly smooth ice cream.

Add the juice from 2 of the lemons and blitz again, this time to dissolve the sugar. Pour this mixture into the cream and combine thoroughly. Leave to chill in the refrigerator for at least an hour.

To make the praline, line a baking tray with baking parchment. Mix the almonds, fennel seeds and salt together. Put the sugar and water in a small saucepan. Simmer on a low heat, stirring carefully until the sugar has dissolved, then turn up the heat and allow the syrup to bubble until it is a light golden brown – at this point it will be on the verge of turning a deeper colour and will be in danger of burning. Remove from the heat immediately and stir in the almond mixture. Tip out onto the lined baking tray and spread it out as much as possible. Leave to cool, by which point it will be hard and brittle. Break into chunks.

Taste the chilled cream mixture and add a little more lemon juice if you think it needs it. Churn in an ice-cream maker until thick, smooth and aerated. Stir around half the praline (save the rest for another occasion) through the ice cream at this point, and churn for a further minute. Scrape into a freezer container and freeze. Remove from the freezer 10 minutes before you want to serve it.

DRIZZLE CAKE WITH A TWIST

Serves 10–12

250g/1 cup plus 2 tbsp
  unsalted butter, softened,
  plus extra for greasing

200g/1 cup caster
  (superfine) sugar

Finely grated zest and juice
  of 2 mandarins

Finely grated zest of 1 lime

3 large eggs

300g/2¼ cups self-raising
  (self-rising) flour

For the syrup

Finely grated zest and juice
  of 2 limes

Finely grated zest and juice
  of 2 mandarins

150g/about 1 cup icing
  (confectioners') sugar

1 tbsp tequila (optional)

This is probably the cake I make more than any other,
but it is rarely the same twice. The basic recipe is very
reliable and lends itself to all kinds of flavour variations.
The traditionally subtle addition of lemon is wonderful,
but this is my absolute favourite – mandarin and lime,
with a tequila-spiked syrup.

Preheat the oven to 170°C/340°F/Gas mark 3½. Butter a
large (900g/2lb) loaf tin and line it with baking parchment.

Cream the butter, sugar and citrus zests together until very
pale, fluffy and increased in volume. Add the eggs one at a
time, along with 2 tablespoons of the flour, then incorporate
the remaining flour. Using a light hand, mix in the
mandarin juice – you should have a batter with a reluctant
dropping consistency.

Scrape into the loaf tin, then bake in the oven for
approximately 1 hour – it is done when it has slightly
shrunk away from the sides and a skewer comes out clean.

While the cake is baking, make the syrup. Put the zests,
juices and sugar into a saucepan and warm through gently
on a low heat until the sugar has dissolved. Stir in the
tequila, if using.

Pierce the cake all over with a cocktail stick or similar, then
pour over the syrup, trying to make sure most of it goes into
the centre of the cake, rather than around the edges. Leave
the cake to cool in the tin until it is completely cold.

RUM AND MARMALADE
LOAF CAKE

Serves 10–12

175g/⅓ cup plus 1 tsp butter, softened, plus extra for greasing

100g/¾ cup raisins

100ml/7 tbsp rum

175g/1⅓ cups wholemeal (wholewheat) spelt flour

2 tsp baking powder

1 tsp ground ginger

1 tsp ground mixed spice

175g/¾ cup plus 2 tbsp dark muscovado sugar

Finely grated zest of 1 lime

150g/½ cup marmalade

3 eggs

50g/⅓ cup finely chopped stem ginger

To glaze

2 tbsp marmalade

1 tbsp rum (optional)

A good keeping cake this, if wrapped up well and left somewhere dark. You can use any marmalade to make this.

Preheat the oven to 180°C/350°F/Gas mark 4. Butter and line a 1kg/2-lb loaf tin.

Put the raisins in a small saucepan and add the rum. Bring to the boil, then immediately remove from the heat and leave to stand while you make the rest of the cake.

Put the flour in a bowl with the baking powder and spices. Whisk together to combine and remove any lumps.

Beat the butter and sugar together in another bowl with the lime zest until very soft, and lightened to the colour of butterscotch. Beat in the marmalade, then add the eggs one at a time, adding a couple of tablespoons of the flour mixture with each addition until it is all combined. Stir through the rum-infused raisins and the stem ginger along with any liquid that hasn't been absorbed.

Scrape the mixture into the prepared loaf tin and bake in the oven for around 1 hour, until well risen and a rich brown. For the glaze, melt the marmalade and rum, if using, together in a small saucepan and brush over the cake while it is still warm. Leave to cool in the tin. If you can bear to wrap this up and leave it for a couple of days, it will be all the better for it.

ORANGE AND GINGER
BUTTER SHORTBREAD

Makes 8 slices

150g/¾ cup golden caster (superfine) sugar

250g/1¾ cups plus 2 tbsp plain (all-purpose) flour

75g/2½oz ground almonds

A pinch of salt

Finely grated zest of 1 orange or grapefruit

200g/¾ cup plus 2 tbsp butter, softened

1 egg yolk, plus 1 whole egg, beaten, to glaze

50g/2½ tbsp stem ginger

50g/2½ tbsp finely chopped candied citrus peel (orange or grapefruit)

50g/2½ tbsp pine nuts

Icing (confectioners') sugar, for dusting

Variation

The ginger version packs a punch, but for something sweeter and more mellow, just omit the ginger and add around a teaspoon of orange blossom water with the egg. Keep the candied peel and pine nuts!

This is a lovely buttery shortbread, studded with stem ginger and candied peel – I use orange or grapefruit here, but you can use any you prefer; lemon is good too. It is based on the Dutch shortbread *Boterkoek*, which I first came across in Gaitri Pagrach-Chandra's wonderful *Warm Bread and Honey Cake*.

Put the sugar, flour and ground almonds in a large bowl and add the salt. Whisk to combine and remove any lumps. Add the zest, butter, egg yolk, stem ginger, citrus peel and pine nuts, and lightly knead everything together until you have a dough.

Shape the dough into a fairly flat round, then either lightly roll out or press into a 24cm/9½-in round tin. Chill well in the refrigerator, preferably overnight, then bring back to room temperature. Preheat the oven to 180°C/350°F/Gas mark 4.

Score lines in the dough to mark out 8 portions. Brush with the beaten egg and bake in the oven for 25–30 minutes. The dough should colour only very lightly, if at all, and should still be soft when it comes out of the oven. Leave to cool, then dust with icing (confectioners') sugar and cut into slices, following the score lines you marked before baking. Store in an airtight tin.

PRESERVES AND DRINKS

CHEAT'S PRESERVED LEMONS (OR LIMES, OR ORANGES ...)

4 lemons (or any other
type of citrus)

1 tsp sea salt

And here is one recipe I absolutely could not do without. It is an instant version of preserved lemons I discovered in Anna Hansen's *The Modern Pantry* cookbook and it's a brilliant way of getting that potent, salty burst of citrus into dishes when you haven't homemade preserved lemons to hand or you don't want to shell out for the generally substandard and ridiculously expensive bought variety. And actually, I find this version brighter and more versatile – the juice is salty, but not overly so, and has an intense, citrusy flavour which makes it ideal in dressings or just drizzled over some fish or chicken to brighten it up. I have made this with Seville oranges, blood oranges, mandarins (tricky because of the thin mandarin skin but do-able; just accept that you need to scrape pith from the inside, rather than pare zest from the outside), limes and grapefruit. All wonderful. Citrus preserved this way will keep indefinitely in the refrigerator, but will gradually lose its vibrancy of colour. To preserve it for longer, you can freeze it.

Pare the zest from the lemons in large slices, preferably with a swivel peeler, then trim off any excess white pith. Put in a small saucepan, squeeze the pared lemons and add the juice to the pan along with the sea salt. Bring to the boil, then turn down the heat and simmer for around 10 minutes or until the zest is tender.

Allow to cool and keep in a sterilized jar in the refrigerator until needed. It will keep for months, but can be used immediately.

CANDIED CITRUS ZEST

1–2 citrus fruit

100g/½ cup
  granulated sugar

150ml/10 tbsp water

To store

About 75g/6 tbsp
  granulated sugar

¼–½ tsp citric acid
  (optional)

This is a very quick way of preserving zest – the process is sped up because you are using just the pared zest, not the pith. It is one of those things you will not be able to stop eating – the flavour is intense and, if you add the citric acid, mouth-numbingly addictive. I use it as a garnish, or simply as a sweet (there is always a tub of these on my kitchen worktop). I will also finely chop it or blitz it to a powder to sprinkle or to give a sherbety hit.

Pare the zest from the fruit in thick strips – don't worry if a little pith is attached to the zest, this is to be expected. Slice the strips thinly, just slightly thicker than you would get if you used a parer.

Put the zest in a small saucepan and cover with cold water. Bring to the boil then immediately strain. Run under cold water, then repeat the process. Set aside the drained zest while you make the sugar syrup.

Put the sugar and water in a saucepan. Heat slowly, stirring until the sugar has completely dissolved. Add the zest and bring to the boil. Turn down and simmer gently for 10–15 minutes until the zest is translucent.

Remove the zest from the syrup with a slotted spoon and spread out on kitchen paper or a piece of baking parchment. Leave to dry for around an hour.

To store, sprinkle with sugar and keep in an airtight container. What I normally do is pound a little citric acid in a pestle and mortar until it is as powdery as icing (confectioners') sugar, and mix this with the sugar – it will make the flavours pop and will really enhance the sour qualities of the zest.

continued...

Tip

The leftover syrup can also be used for syrup or sweets.
Add some citrus juice and simmer for a few minutes to
make a syrup for desserts and ice cream, or to pour over
ice chips. And if you have a sugar thermometer, you can
then use this syrup to make sweets: simply heat until it
reaches 149°C/300°F, then pour onto some greased baking
parchment. It will cool quickly – when it is cool enough to
touch, pick it up in one large piece and work/pull it into
a rope. Fold it back on itself and twist, then repeat until it
feels as though it is too firm to continue without it snapping
– you want to end up with a long twist around 1.5cm/½-in
thick. Then cut it into sweets with scissors or a sharp knife.

YUZUKOSHO AND OTHER KOSHOS

For lemon-mandarin-kosho

15g/½oz finely grated lemon zest (from around 4 large lemons)

5g/⅙oz finely grated mandarin zest (from around 4 mandarins)

40g/1½oz medium-hot red chillies, deseeded and finely chopped

6g/¼oz salt

For lime-Scotch bonnet-kosho

20g/¾oz finely grated lime zest

5g/⅙oz Scotch bonnet chilli, deseeded and finely chopped

35g/1¼oz mild-medium-hot red or green chillies, deseeded and finely chopped

6g/¼oz salt

This is a Japanese condiment made from very finely chopped yuzu zest and chilli. It's hot, salty, very sour but with floral notes coming through that really lift it. As it is very difficult to buy fresh yuzu, if you want an authentic yuzukosho, you will probably need to buy it ready-made. However, I have found that you can use the same principles and adapt them to other kinds of chilli and citrus, which is what I've done here. If you are lucky enough to find some fresh yuzu, remember that the basic formula is four times the amount of chilli to zest. Then weigh and add 10 per cent of the final weight in salt. This formula can be messed around with as much as you like, depending on the type of chillies you use, with the chilli/zest ratio very adaptable. However, the salt must always be 10 per cent of the total.

To prepare, simply put everything in a food processor or grind with a pestle and mortar. It tastes good from the start, but try to leave it in the refrigerator to ferment gently for a week and the flavour will be vastly improved. After that, it will keep indefinitely.

Here are a couple of examples of my favourite mixes, making relatively small amounts – a little does go a long way, though.

continued...

Lemon-mandarin-kosho

When you can get very fragrant mandarins, around February/March time, the flavour of this version can be wonderfully complex and subtle for such a punch-packing condiment.

Lime-Scotch bonnet-kosho

Good for adding a hot/sour note to sweet coconut milk dishes. If you want to make this very hot, just increase the amount of Scotch bonnet chilli and reduce the amount of mild – I have included just a small amount for flavour as opposed to heat.

Once you have some kosho stored in the refrigerator, you can use it in any number of ways. I use it in its pure form as a condiment for soup, or spread on grilled meat or fish. You can turn it into a thinner sauce with some lime juice and a pinch of sugar or honey, and it makes an incredible dipping sauce with soy sauce and juice. You can add other aromatics to it such as garlic and ginger. And if you need to offset the sweetness from other ingredients in your dish, add this kosho to an oil-based dressing – for example, try it with the sweetest, height-of-the-season tomatoes.

LEMONADE

**Makes about
1 litre/2 pints**

4 lemons (or 6 limes, or 3
lemons and 2 limes)

100–150g/½–¾ cup caster
(superfine) sugar, to taste

1 litre/scant 4 cups water,
or a mixture of water
and sparkling water

**This recipe works just as well with limes or with a
combination of lemons and limes, as limes add a sherbety
element to the flavour. This is a quick version as no
steeping is necessary. It is lovely garnished with citrus
slices, cucumber slices, mint leaves and borage flowers,
and is also good with a slug of vodka, gin, or if using
limes, rum.**

Roughly chop the half the citrus and put in a food
processor. Finely grate the zest and squeeze the juice of the
remaining fruit. Add to the food processor with the sugar
(go for the lower quantity if you prefer it sharp, more if you
have a sweet tooth) and 240ml/1 cup of the water and blitz
until everything is finely chopped. You should find the sugar
has dissolved.

Strain through a sieve into a large jug with plenty of ice, and
top with the remaining water or sparkling water. Add more
sugar to taste, if needed.

The Quickest Version

This is a very quick and easy drink, found wherever you get
fresh limes. Simply take the juice of 2 limes, mix with ½ tsp
sugar, slightly more of salt and top with sparkling water. I
like to add a dash of bitters as well. I am told it makes a very
good hangover cure – as a friend of mine says: "Like your
own electrolyte sachet but nicer."

Preserved Lemonade

This is unbelievably refreshing. It is based on a Vietnamese
recipe, and you can use any citrus which has been preserved
the traditional way – I really love limequats for this, but
lemons, limes and sour oranges are all good. It is very
simple. Put ¼–½ preserved lemon or similar in a glass
along with some granulated sugar – start with a couple of
teaspoons. Muddle it all together to release the juices from
the citrus, then top with sparkling water. Taste and adjust
the sweetness levels if necessary. Try adding cucumber slices
for sharp contrast or add a measure of rum or vodka for
something alcoholic.

INDEX

almond and fennel praline 90
asparagus, linguine with lemon and 54
aubergines, grilled with mozzarella and yuzukosho 46–48

beef carpaccio salad 26
bergamot and rose Turkish delight pavlova 86
biscuits: orange and ginger butter shortbread 96
blackberry, orange and orange blossom clafoutis 75–77
broccoli, mandarin chicken with giant couscous and charred 40–42
burrata, blood orange and freekeh salad 23

cakes: drizzle cake with a twist 93
    rum and marmalade loaf cake 94
candied citrus zest 103–104
caramelized potatoes with orange 63
cardamom, blood orange tarte Tatin 80–82
carpaccio: beef carpaccio salad 26
cauliflower, roasted with lemon, nigella seeds and gremolata 69
ceviche, sea bass 14–16
chard, chicken and giant couscous soup 9–10
cheat's preserved lemons 100
cheese: grilled aubergines with mozzarella and yuzukosho 46–48
roast vegetables with feta and orange 56
chicken: chicken, chard and giant couscous soup 9–10

coconut, lime and lemongrass chicken salad 17–19
lime and chicken tortilla soup 6–8
mandarin chicken with giant couscous and charred broccoli 40–42
marinated chicken with charred limes, saffron butter and soft flatbreads 43–45
chicory braised with grapefruit, mandarin and soy 65
chillies: lemon-mandarin-kosho 105–106
lime-Scotch bonnet-kosho 105–106
marinated squid, smoked chilli, fennel and lemon salad 24
tomatillo, grapefruit and chilli salsa 50
cinnamon, rolls, orange pecan and 83–85
citrus: citrus butter sauce 38
citrus slices, deep-fried 11–13
clafoutis, blackberry, orange and orange blossom 75–77
coconut: coconut, lime and lemongrass chicken salad 17–19
dal with lemon or lime curry 51–53
couscous: chicken, chard and giant couscous soup 9–10
mandarin chicken with giant couscous 40–42
crème anglaise: blood orange and cardamom tarte Tatin 80–82
curry, dal with lemon or lime 51–53

dauphinoise, fennel and lemon 60
drying citrus zest 75

fennel: almond and fennel praline 90

fennel and lemon dauphinoise 60
marinated squid, smoked chilli, fennel and lemon salad 24
feta, roast vegetables with orange 56
fish: fish tacos 48–50
sea bass ceviche 14–16
spiced sea bass with citrus butter sauce 38
whole baked fish with lemon and ouzo 32–34
freekeh, blood orange and burrata salad 23

grapefruit: gin and bitter grapefruit granita 88
chicory braised with grapefruit, mandarin and soy 65
tomatillo, grapefruit and chilli salsa 50
gin and bitter grapefruit granita 88
gremolata 69

ice cream: lemon ice cream with almond and fennel praline 90

Jerusalem artichoke and preserved orange salad 28

kosho 105–106
lemon-mandarin-kosho 105–106
lemon-mandarin-kosho dressing 26
lime-Scotch bonnet-kosho 105–106
kumquats: Sussex pond puddings 78

lemongrass, coconut, lime and chicken salad 17–19
lemons: dal with lemon or lime curry 51–53
fennel and lemon dauphinoise 60

lemon-mandarin-kosho 105–106
lemon-mandarin-kosho dressing 26
lemon pizzette 20
lemonade 108
linguine with lemon and asparagus 54
marinated squid, smoked chilli, fennel and lemon salad 24
preserved lemonade 108
preserved lemons, cheat's 100
roast tomatoes with lemon and lemon thyme 67
roasted cauliflower with lemon, nigella seeds and gremolata 69
whole baked fish with lemon and ouzo 32–34
limes: coconut, lime and lemongrass chicken salad 17–19
drizzle cake with a twist 93
lime and chicken tortilla soup 6–8
lime-pickled red onions 45
lime-Scotch bonnet-kosho 105–106
marinated chicken with charred limes, saffron butter and soft flatbreads 43–45
preserved limes, cheat's 100
limequats: Sussex pond puddings 78
preserved lemonade 108

mandarins: chicory braised with grapefruit, mandarin and soy 65
drizzle cake with a twist 93
lemon-mandarin-kosho 105–106
lemon-mandarin-kosho dressing 26
mandarin chicken 40–42
ponzu 35–36
marmalade: rum and marmalade loaf cake 94
Sussex pond puddings 78

meringues: bergamot and rose Turkish delight pavlova 86
blood orange and rhubarb meringue pie 72–74
mung beans: dal 51–53

onions, lime-pickled red 45
oranges: blackberry, orange and orange blossom clafoutis 75–77
blood orange and cardamom tarte Tatin 80–82
blood orange and rhubarb meringue pie 72–74
blood orange, burrata and freekeh salad 23
caramelized potatoes with orange 63
Jerusalem artichoke and preserved orange salad 28
orange and ginger butter shortbread 96
orange, pecan and cinnamon rolls 83–85
preserved oranges, cheat's 100
roast vegetables with feta and orange 56
rum and marmalade loaf cake 94
sea bass ceviche 14–16
ouzo, whole baked fish with lemon and 32–34

pasta: linguine with lemon and asparagus 54
pavlova, bergamot and rose Turkish delight 86
pecan, orange and cinnamon rolls 83–85
pie, blood orange and rhubarb meringue 72–74
pizzette, lemon 20
ponzu 35–36
pork: tonkatsu with yuzu coleslaw and ponzu 35–36
potatoes: caramelized potatoes with orange 63
praline, almond and fennel 90
preserves 99–109
puddings, Sussex pond 78

rhubarb meringue pie, blood orange and 72–74
rolls, orange, pecan and cinnamon 83–85
roast vegetables with feta and orange 56
rum, marmalade loaf cake 94

saffron butter 43–45
salads 17–19, 23, 24, 26, 28
salsa: avocado salsa 50
tomatillo, grapefruit and chilli salsa 50
sausages: lemon pizzette 20
sea bass: sea bass ceviche 14–16
spiced sea bass with citrus butter sauce 38
whole baked fish with lemon and ouzo 32–34
shortbread, orange and ginger butter 96
small plates 11–13, 14–16, 20
soups 6–8, 9–10
squid, marinated with smoked chilli, fennel and lemon salad 24
Sussex pond puddings 78

tacos, fish 48–50
tarts: blood orange and cardamom tarte Tatin 80–82
tequila syrup 93
tomatoes, roast with lemon 67
tonkatsu with yuzu coleslaw and ponzu 35–36
tortilla soup, lime and chicken 6–8
Turkish delight, bergamot and rose pavlova 86

yuzu: yuzu coleslaw 35–36
yuzukosho 105–106
yuzukosho 105–106
grilled aubergines with mozzarella and yuzukosho 46–48

zest: candied citrus zest 103–104

ACKNOWLEDGEMENTS

A trio of brilliant people helped to get this book off the ground. Ed Griffiths helped me to realise that my love of citrus would translate well into a book – and gave me some very good advice along the way, particularly on Japanese food. Clare Hulton, my wonderful agent, believed in the book, as did my equally wonderful editor, Sarah Lavelle. Thank you all and extra thanks to Sarah for being so patient with me during the writing process.

Thanks to the supremely talented team on the photoshoot: Mowie Kay, Iris Bromet, Laurie Perry, Katie Marshall and especially Marina Filippelli. I couldn't be happier with the results.

Thank you to everyone at Quadrille, especially Emily Lapworth for the beautiful design and stunning cover. Thank you also to Sally Somers for making the copy-editing process so painless. And to Sofie Shearman, for pulling it all together so brilliantly.

So many fellow food writers, friends and family helped me during the writing of this book. Xanthe Clay sent me Makrut limes, finger limes and even yuzu from Japan. Sally Butcher and her husband Jamshid were incredibly hospitable and helpful on the role of citrus in the Middle East. Kerstin Rogers sent me numerous citrus-related links, Tim Hayward gave advice on citrus and knives and Charlie Hicks helped me on availability and seasonality. Both Fiona Kirkpatrick and Alanna Lauder gave me tips on citrus drinks. Naomi Hourihane came to my rescue with rosemary flowers.

Jinny Johnson was always at the other end of the phone, giving advice but often just letting me think out loud.

Special thanks to my mother, who taught me to cook from first principles and who during the course of this book, brainstormed with me, searched out old recipes and sent me ingredients to play with, including citrus leaves from her trees in Greece.

Finally, as always, thanks to Shariq, Lilly and Adam, who get better at constructive criticism with every book I write and who are a pleasure to cook for. Stellar testers, all.